Pray

DATE _____

TODAY'S PASSAGE   PREACHER   SERMON TOPIC

NOTES

KEY VERSES

KEY POINTS

PRAYER

APPLICATION

Prayer journal

DATE _____

TODAY'S PASSAGE   PREACHER   SERMON TOPIC

NOTES

PRAYER

KEY VERSES

KEY POINTS

APPLICATION

Prayer journal

DATE _____

TODAY'S PASSAGE   PREACHER   SERMON TOPIC

NOTES

_____

KEY VERSES

PRAYER

_____

KEY POINTS

APPLICATION

Prayer journal

DATE _____

TODAY'S PASSAGE _____ PREACHER _____ SERMON TOPIC _____

NOTES
_____
_____
_____
_____
_____
_____
_____
_____
_____

PRAYER
_____
_____
_____
_____
_____
_____
_____
_____
_____
_____
_____
_____
_____

KEY VERSES

KEY POINTS

APPLICATION

Prayer journal

DATE

TODAY'S PASSAGE   PREACHER   SERMON TOPIC

NOTES

KEY VERSES

KEY POINTS

PRAYER

APPLICATION

Prayer journal

DATE _____

TODAY'S PASSAGE _____   PREACHER _____   SERMON TOPIC _____

NOTES

KEY VERSES

PRAYER

KEY POINTS

APPLICATION

Prayer journal

DATE _____

TODAY'S PASSAGE   PREACHER   SERMON TOPIC

NOTES

| KEY VERSES |

| KEY POINTS |

PRAYER

| APPLICATION |

Prayer journal

DATE _____

TODAY'S PASSAGE   PREACHER   SERMON TOPIC

NOTES

KEY VERSES

PRAYER

KEY POINTS

APPLICATION

Prayer journal

DATE

TODAY'S PASSAGE   PREACHER   SERMON TOPIC

NOTES

| KEY VERSES |

PRAYER

| KEY POINTS |

| APPLICATION |

Prayer journal

DATE _____

TODAY'S PASSAGE　　　PREACHER　　　SERMON TOPIC

NOTES

_____

_____

_____

_____

_____

_____

_____

_____

_____

_____

_____

PRAYER

_____

_____

_____

_____

_____

_____

_____

_____

_____

_____

_____

_____

_____

_____

_____

_____

KEY VERSES

KEY POINTS

APPLICATION

Prayer journal

DATE

TODAY'S PASSAGE   PREACHER   SERMON TOPIC

NOTES

KEY VERSES

PRAYER

KEY POINTS

APPLICATION

Prayer journal

DATE _____

TODAY'S PASSAGE _____   PREACHER _____   SERMON TOPIC _____

NOTES

_____
_____
_____
_____
_____
_____
_____
_____
_____
_____

PRAYER

_____
_____
_____
_____
_____
_____
_____
_____
_____
_____
_____
_____
_____
_____

KEY VERSES

KEY POINTS

APPLICATION

Prayer journal

DATE

TODAY'S PASSAGE PREACHER SERMON TOPIC

NOTES

KEY VERSES

KEY POINTS

PRAYER

APPLICATION

Prayer journal

DATE

TODAY'S PASSAGE   PREACHER   SERMON TOPIC

NOTES

KEY VERSES

PRAYER

KEY POINTS

APPLICATION

Prayer journal

DATE

TODAY'S PASSAGE   PREACHER   SERMON TOPIC

NOTES

KEY VERSES

KEY POINTS

PRAYER

APPLICATION

Prayer journal

DATE

TODAY'S PASSAGE   PREACHER   SERMON TOPIC

NOTES

PRAYER

KEY VERSES

KEY POINTS

APPLICATION

Prayer journal

DATE _____

TODAY'S PASSAGE   PREACHER   SERMON TOPIC

NOTES _____

_____
_____
_____
_____
_____
_____
_____
_____
_____
_____
_____
_____

PRAYER _____

_____
_____
_____
_____
_____
_____
_____
_____
_____
_____
_____
_____
_____
_____

KEY VERSES

KEY POINTS

APPLICATION

Prayer journal

DATE

TODAY'S PASSAGE   PREACHER   SERMON TOPIC

NOTES

PRAYER

KEY VERSES

KEY POINTS

APPLICATION

Prayer journal

DATE _____

TODAY'S PASSAGE   PREACHER   SERMON TOPIC

NOTES

KEY VERSES

KEY POINTS

PRAYER

APPLICATION

Prayer journal

DATE _____

TODAY'S PASSAGE   PREACHER   SERMON TOPIC

NOTES

KEY VERSES

PRAYER

KEY POINTS

APPLICATION

Prayer journal

DATE _____

TODAY'S PASSAGE   PREACHER   SERMON TOPIC

NOTES

| KEY VERSES |

| KEY POINTS |

PRAYER

| APPLICATION |

Prayer journal

DATE

TODAY'S PASSAGE   PREACHER   SERMON TOPIC

NOTES

KEY VERSES

PRAYER

KEY POINTS

APPLICATION

Prayer journal

DATE _____

TODAY'S PASSAGE   PREACHER   SERMON TOPIC

NOTES

KEY VERSES

KEY POINTS

PRAYER

APPLICATION

Prayer journal

DATE _____

TODAY'S PASSAGE　　　PREACHER　　　SERMON TOPIC

NOTES

KEY VERSES

PRAYER

KEY POINTS

APPLICATION

Prayer journal

DATE

TODAY'S PASSAGE   PREACHER   SERMON TOPIC

NOTES

KEY VERSES

KEY POINTS

PRAYER

APPLICATION

Prayer journal

DATE

TODAY'S PASSAGE   PREACHER   SERMON TOPIC

NOTES

KEY VERSES

PRAYER

KEY POINTS

APPLICATION

Prayer journal

DATE _____

TODAY'S PASSAGE   PREACHER   SERMON TOPIC

NOTES

KEY VERSES

KEY POINTS

PRAYER

APPLICATION

Prayer journal

DATE

TODAY'S PASSAGE PREACHER SERMON TOPIC

NOTES

| KEY VERSES |

| KEY POINTS |

PRAYER

| APPLICATION |

Prayer journal

DATE _____

TODAY'S PASSAGE   PREACHER   SERMON TOPIC

NOTES

KEY VERSES

KEY POINTS

PRAYER

APPLICATION

Prayer journal

DATE

TODAY'S PASSAGE   PREACHER   SERMON TOPIC

NOTES

KEY VERSES

PRAYER

KEY POINTS

APPLICATION

Prayer journal

DATE _____

TODAY'S PASSAGE   PREACHER   SERMON TOPIC

NOTES

PRAYER

KEY VERSES

KEY POINTS

APPLICATION

Prayer journal

DATE _____

TODAY'S PASSAGE   PREACHER   SERMON TOPIC

NOTES
_____
_____
_____
_____
_____
_____
_____
_____
_____

PRAYER
_____
_____
_____
_____
_____
_____
_____
_____
_____
_____
_____
_____
_____

KEY VERSES

KEY POINTS

APPLICATION

Prayer journal

DATE

TODAY'S PASSAGE   PREACHER   SERMON TOPIC

NOTES

KEY VERSES

KEY POINTS

PRAYER

APPLICATION

Prayer journal

DATE

TODAY'S PASSAGE PREACHER SERMON TOPIC

NOTES

PRAYER

KEY VERSES

KEY POINTS

APPLICATION

Prayer journal

DATE

TODAY'S PASSAGE PREACHER SERMON TOPIC

NOTES

PRAYER

KEY VERSES

KEY POINTS

APPLICATION

Prayer journal

DATE: _____

TODAY'S PASSAGE PREACHER SERMON TOPIC

NOTES
_____
_____
_____
_____
_____
_____
_____
_____
_____
_____

PRAYER
_____
_____
_____
_____
_____
_____
_____
_____
_____
_____
_____

KEY VERSES

KEY POINTS

APPLICATION

Prayer journal

DATE _____

TODAY'S PASSAGE   PREACHER   SERMON TOPIC

NOTES

KEY VERSES

PRAYER

KEY POINTS

APPLICATION

Prayer journal

DATE

TODAY'S PASSAGE

PREACHER

SERMON TOPIC

NOTES

KEY VERSES

PRAYER

KEY POINTS

APPLICATION

Prayer journal

DATE _____

TODAY'S PASSAGE PREACHER SERMON TOPIC

NOTES

_____

_____

_____

_____

_____

_____

_____

_____

_____

_____

_____

_____

PRAYER

_____

_____

_____

_____

_____

_____

_____

_____

_____

_____

_____

_____

_____

_____

_____

KEY VERSES

KEY POINTS

APPLICATION

Prayer journal

DATE _____

TODAY'S PASSAGE   PREACHER   SERMON TOPIC

NOTES

_____
_____
_____
_____
_____
_____
_____
_____
_____
_____

PRAYER

_____
_____
_____
_____
_____
_____
_____
_____
_____
_____
_____
_____
_____

KEY VERSES

KEY POINTS

APPLICATION

Prayer journal

DATE _____

TODAY'S PASSAGE   PREACHER   SERMON TOPIC

NOTES
_____
_____
_____
_____
_____
_____
_____
_____
_____
_____
_____
_____
_____

PRAYER
_____
_____
_____
_____
_____
_____
_____
_____
_____
_____
_____
_____
_____
_____
_____
_____
_____

KEY VERSES

KEY POINTS

APPLICATION

Prayer journal

DATE

TODAY'S PASSAGE　　　PREACHER　　　SERMON TOPIC

NOTES

PRAYER

KEY VERSES

KEY POINTS

APPLICATION

Prayer journal

DATE

TODAY'S PASSAGE   PREACHER   SERMON TOPIC

NOTES

PRAYER

KEY VERSES

KEY POINTS

APPLICATION

Prayer journal

DATE

TODAY'S PASSAGE   PREACHER   SERMON TOPIC

NOTES

KEY VERSES

PRAYER

KEY POINTS

APPLICATION

Prayer journal

DATE

TODAY'S PASSAGE PREACHER SERMON TOPIC

NOTES

KEY VERSES

PRAYER

KEY POINTS

APPLICATION

Prayer journal

DATE

TODAY'S PASSAGE   PREACHER   SERMON TOPIC

NOTES

KEY VERSES

PRAYER

KEY POINTS

APPLICATION

Prayer journal

DATE

TODAY'S PASSAGE   PREACHER   SERMON TOPIC

NOTES

| KEY VERSES |

PRAYER

| KEY POINTS |

| APPLICATION |

Prayer journal

DATE

TODAY'S PASSAGE   PREACHER   SERMON TOPIC

NOTES

KEY VERSES

PRAYER

KEY POINTS

APPLICATION

Prayer journal

DATE _____

TODAY'S PASSAGE   PREACHER   SERMON TOPIC

NOTES

KEY VERSES

KEY POINTS

PRAYER

APPLICATION

Prayer journal

DATE

TODAY'S PASSAGE PREACHER SERMON TOPIC

NOTES

KEY VERSES

PRAYER

KEY POINTS

APPLICATION

Prayer journal

DATE _____

TODAY'S PASSAGE   PREACHER   SERMON TOPIC

NOTES

KEY VERSES

PRAYER

KEY POINTS

APPLICATION

Prayer journal

DATE

TODAY'S PASSAGE   PREACHER   SERMON TOPIC

NOTES

| KEY VERSES |

| KEY POINTS |

PRAYER

| APPLICATION |

Prayer journal

DATE

TODAY'S PASSAGE   PREACHER   SERMON TOPIC

NOTES

| KEY VERSES |

| KEY POINTS |

PRAYER

| APPLICATION |

Prayer journal

DATE

TODAY'S PASSAGE   PREACHER   SERMON TOPIC

NOTES

| KEY VERSES |

PRAYER

| KEY POINTS |

| APPLICATION |

Prayer journal

DATE

TODAY'S PASSAGE   PREACHER   SERMON TOPIC

NOTES

KEY VERSES

KEY POINTS

PRAYER

APPLICATION

Prayer journal

DATE

TODAY'S PASSAGE   PREACHER   SERMON TOPIC

NOTES

PRAYER

KEY VERSES

KEY POINTS

APPLICATION

Prayer journal

DATE

TODAY'S PASSAGE   PREACHER   SERMON TOPIC

NOTES

KEY VERSES

PRAYER

KEY POINTS

APPLICATION

Prayer journal

DATE _____

TODAY'S PASSAGE   PREACHER   SERMON TOPIC

NOTES

KEY VERSES

PRAYER

KEY POINTS

APPLICATION

Prayer journal

DATE

TODAY'S PASSAGE   PREACHER   SERMON TOPIC

NOTES

KEY VERSES

KEY POINTS

PRAYER

APPLICATION

Prayer journal

DATE _____

TODAY'S PASSAGE   PREACHER   SERMON TOPIC

NOTES

_____
_____
_____
_____
_____
_____
_____
_____
_____
_____

PRAYER

_____
_____
_____
_____
_____
_____
_____
_____
_____
_____
_____
_____
_____
_____
_____

KEY VERSES

KEY POINTS

APPLICATION

Prayer journal

DATE

TODAY'S PASSAGE   PREACHER   SERMON TOPIC

NOTES

PRAYER

KEY VERSES

KEY POINTS

APPLICATION

Prayer journal

DATE

TODAY'S PASSAGE   PREACHER   SERMON TOPIC

NOTES

PRAYER

KEY VERSES

KEY POINTS

APPLICATION

Prayer journal

DATE

TODAY'S PASSAGE   PREACHER   SERMON TOPIC

NOTES

KEY VERSES

PRAYER

KEY POINTS

APPLICATION

Prayer journal

DATE

TODAY'S PASSAGE   PREACHER   SERMON TOPIC

NOTES

KEY VERSES

PRAYER

KEY POINTS

APPLICATION

Prayer journal

DATE _____

TODAY'S PASSAGE   PREACHER   SERMON TOPIC

NOTES
_____
_____
_____
_____
_____
_____
_____
_____
_____
_____
_____
_____
_____

PRAYER
_____
_____
_____
_____
_____
_____
_____
_____
_____
_____
_____
_____
_____
_____
_____

KEY VERSES

KEY POINTS

APPLICATION

Prayer journal

DATE

TODAY'S PASSAGE PREACHER SERMON TOPIC

NOTES

KEY VERSES

PRAYER

KEY POINTS

APPLICATION

Prayer journal

DATE

TODAY'S PASSAGE   PREACHER   SERMON TOPIC

NOTES

KEY VERSES

PRAYER

KEY POINTS

APPLICATION

Prayer journal

DATE

TODAY'S PASSAGE PREACHER SERMON TOPIC

NOTES

KEY VERSES

PRAYER

KEY POINTS

APPLICATION

Prayer journal

DATE _____

TODAY'S PASSAGE   PREACHER   SERMON TOPIC

NOTES

| KEY VERSES |

| KEY POINTS |

PRAYER

| APPLICATION |

Prayer journal

DATE _____

TODAY'S PASSAGE   PREACHER   SERMON TOPIC

NOTES

KEY VERSES

PRAYER

KEY POINTS

APPLICATION

Prayer journal

DATE _____

TODAY'S PASSAGE _____ PREACHER _____ SERMON TOPIC _____

NOTES

_____
_____
_____
_____
_____
_____
_____
_____
_____
_____
_____

PRAYER

_____
_____
_____
_____
_____
_____
_____
_____
_____
_____
_____
_____
_____
_____
_____

KEY VERSES

KEY POINTS

APPLICATION

Prayer journal

DATE _____

TODAY'S PASSAGE   PREACHER   SERMON TOPIC

NOTES

_____
_____
_____
_____
_____
_____
_____
_____
_____
_____

KEY VERSES

PRAYER

_____
_____
_____
_____
_____
_____
_____

KEY POINTS

_____
_____
_____
_____
_____
_____
_____
_____

APPLICATION

Prayer journal

DATE _____

TODAY'S PASSAGE   PREACHER   SERMON TOPIC

NOTES

_____
_____
_____
_____
_____
_____
_____
_____
_____
_____
_____
_____

PRAYER

_____
_____
_____
_____
_____
_____
_____
_____
_____
_____
_____
_____
_____
_____
_____
_____

KEY VERSES

KEY POINTS

APPLICATION

Prayer journal

DATE

TODAY'S PASSAGE   PREACHER   SERMON TOPIC

NOTES

KEY VERSES

PRAYER

KEY POINTS

APPLICATION

Prayer journal

DATE

TODAY'S PASSAGE PREACHER SERMON TOPIC

NOTES

KEY VERSES

PRAYER

KEY POINTS

APPLICATION

Prayer journal

DATE

TODAY'S PASSAGE　　　PREACHER　　　SERMON TOPIC

NOTES

KEY VERSES

PRAYER

KEY POINTS

APPLICATION

Prayer journal

DATE _____

TODAY'S PASSAGE   PREACHER   SERMON TOPIC

NOTES

PRAYER

KEY VERSES

KEY POINTS

APPLICATION

Prayer journal

DATE

TODAY'S PASSAGE PREACHER SERMON TOPIC

NOTES

PRAYER

KEY VERSES

KEY POINTS

APPLICATION

Prayer journal

DATE _____

TODAY'S PASSAGE   PREACHER   SERMON TOPIC

NOTES

| KEY VERSES |

| KEY POINTS |

PRAYER

| APPLICATION |

Prayer journal

DATE

TODAY'S PASSAGE   PREACHER   SERMON TOPIC

NOTES

KEY VERSES

PRAYER

KEY POINTS

APPLICATION

Prayer journal

DATE

TODAY'S PASSAGE   PREACHER   SERMON TOPIC

NOTES

| KEY VERSES |

| KEY POINTS |

PRAYER

| APPLICATION |

Prayer journal

DATE

TODAY'S PASSAGE   PREACHER   SERMON TOPIC

NOTES

KEY VERSES

PRAYER

KEY POINTS

APPLICATION

Prayer journal

DATE

TODAY'S PASSAGE   PREACHER   SERMON TOPIC

NOTES

PRAYER

KEY VERSES

KEY POINTS

APPLICATION

Prayer journal

DATE

TODAY'S PASSAGE   PREACHER   SERMON TOPIC

NOTES

PRAYER

KEY VERSES

KEY POINTS

APPLICATION

Prayer journal

DATE _____

TODAY'S PASSAGE   PREACHER   SERMON TOPIC

NOTES

KEY VERSES

KEY POINTS

PRAYER

APPLICATION

Prayer journal

DATE

TODAY'S PASSAGE   PREACHER   SERMON TOPIC

NOTES

KEY VERSES

PRAYER

KEY POINTS

APPLICATION

Prayer journal

DATE _____

TODAY'S PASSAGE   PREACHER   SERMON TOPIC

NOTES

KEY VERSES

KEY POINTS

PRAYER

APPLICATION

Prayer journal

DATE

TODAY'S PASSAGE PREACHER SERMON TOPIC

NOTES

| KEY VERSES |

PRAYER

| KEY POINTS |

| APPLICATION |

Prayer journal

DATE _____

TODAY'S PASSAGE   PREACHER   SERMON TOPIC

NOTES

| KEY VERSES |

| KEY POINTS |

PRAYER

| APPLICATION |

Prayer journal

DATE

TODAY'S PASSAGE   PREACHER   SERMON TOPIC

NOTES

KEY VERSES

PRAYER

KEY POINTS

APPLICATION

Prayer journal

DATE _____

TODAY'S PASSAGE   PREACHER   SERMON TOPIC

NOTES

KEY VERSES

KEY POINTS

PRAYER

APPLICATION

Prayer journal

DATE

TODAY'S PASSAGE   PREACHER   SERMON TOPIC

NOTES

KEY VERSES

PRAYER

KEY POINTS

APPLICATION

Prayer journal

DATE

TODAY'S PASSAGE   PREACHER   SERMON TOPIC

NOTES

KEY VERSES

PRAYER

KEY POINTS

APPLICATION

Prayer journal

DATE

TODAY'S PASSAGE   PREACHER   SERMON TOPIC

NOTES

KEY VERSES

KEY POINTS

PRAYER

APPLICATION

Prayer journal

DATE

TODAY'S PASSAGE   PREACHER   SERMON TOPIC

NOTES

KEY VERSES

PRAYER

KEY POINTS

APPLICATION

Prayer journal

DATE

TODAY'S PASSAGE   PREACHER   SERMON TOPIC

NOTES

| KEY VERSES |

PRAYER

| KEY POINTS |

| APPLICATION |

Prayer journal

DATE

TODAY'S PASSAGE   PREACHER   SERMON TOPIC

NOTES

KEY VERSES

KEY POINTS

PRAYER

APPLICATION

Prayer journal

DATE

TODAY'S PASSAGE PREACHER SERMON TOPIC

NOTES

KEY VERSES

PRAYER

KEY POINTS

APPLICATION

Prayer journal

DATE _____

TODAY'S PASSAGE   PREACHER   SERMON TOPIC

NOTES

_____
_____
_____
_____
_____
_____
_____
_____
_____
_____
_____
_____

PRAYER

_____
_____
_____
_____
_____
_____
_____
_____
_____
_____
_____
_____
_____
_____
_____

KEY VERSES

KEY POINTS

APPLICATION

Prayer journal

DATE

TODAY'S PASSAGE   PREACHER   SERMON TOPIC

NOTES

KEY VERSES

PRAYER

KEY POINTS

APPLICATION

Prayer journal

DATE _____

TODAY'S PASSAGE   PREACHER   SERMON TOPIC

NOTES

KEY VERSES

PRAYER

KEY POINTS

APPLICATION

Prayer journal

DATE

TODAY'S PASSAGE PREACHER SERMON TOPIC

NOTES

PRAYER

KEY VERSES

KEY POINTS

APPLICATION

Prayer journal

DATE _____

TODAY'S PASSAGE   PREACHER   SERMON TOPIC

NOTES

| KEY VERSES |

PRAYER

| KEY POINTS |

| APPLICATION |

Prayer journal

DATE

TODAY'S PASSAGE   PREACHER   SERMON TOPIC

NOTES

KEY VERSES

PRAYER

KEY POINTS

APPLICATION

Prayer journal

DATE _____

TODAY'S PASSAGE PREACHER SERMON TOPIC

NOTES

_____
_____
_____
_____
_____
_____
_____
_____
_____
_____
_____
_____

PRAYER

_____
_____
_____
_____
_____
_____
_____
_____
_____
_____
_____
_____
_____
_____
_____
_____

KEY VERSES

KEY POINTS

APPLICATION

Prayer journal

DATE

TODAY'S PASSAGE   PREACHER   SERMON TOPIC

NOTES

KEY VERSES

PRAYER

KEY POINTS

APPLICATION

Prayer journal

DATE _____

TODAY'S PASSAGE PREACHER SERMON TOPIC

NOTES

_____
_____
_____
_____
_____
_____
_____
_____
_____
_____
_____
_____

PRAYER

_____
_____
_____
_____
_____
_____
_____
_____
_____
_____
_____
_____
_____
_____
_____

KEY VERSES

KEY POINTS

APPLICATION

Prayer journal

DATE

TODAY'S PASSAGE   PREACHER   SERMON TOPIC

NOTES

| KEY VERSES |

PRAYER

| KEY POINTS |

| APPLICATION |

Prayer journal

DATE _____

TODAY'S PASSAGE   PREACHER   SERMON TOPIC

NOTES

_____

KEY VERSES

PRAYER

_____

KEY POINTS

APPLICATION

Prayer journal

DATE

TODAY'S PASSAGE   PREACHER   SERMON TOPIC

NOTES

KEY VERSES

PRAYER

KEY POINTS

APPLICATION

Prayer journal

DATE _____

TODAY'S PASSAGE _____ PREACHER _____ SERMON TOPIC _____

NOTES

| KEY VERSES |

| KEY POINTS |

PRAYER

| APPLICATION |

Prayer journal

DATE

TODAY'S PASSAGE   PREACHER   SERMON TOPIC

NOTES

| KEY VERSES |

| KEY POINTS |

PRAYER

| APPLICATION |

Prayer journal

DATE

TODAY'S PASSAGE   PREACHER   SERMON TOPIC

NOTES

KEY VERSES

KEY POINTS

PRAYER

APPLICATION

Prayer journal

DATE

TODAY'S PASSAGE   PREACHER   SERMON TOPIC

NOTES

KEY VERSES

PRAYER

KEY POINTS

APPLICATION

Prayer journal

DATE _____

TODAY'S PASSAGE   PREACHER   SERMON TOPIC

NOTES

PRAYER

KEY VERSES

KEY POINTS

APPLICATION

Prayer journal

DATE

TODAY'S PASSAGE   PREACHER   SERMON TOPIC

NOTES

KEY VERSES

PRAYER

KEY POINTS

APPLICATION

Prayer journal

DATE

TODAY'S PASSAGE   PREACHER   SERMON TOPIC

NOTES

PRAYER

KEY VERSES

KEY POINTS

APPLICATION

Prayer journal

DATE _____

TODAY'S PASSAGE   PREACHER   SERMON TOPIC

NOTES

KEY VERSES

PRAYER

KEY POINTS

APPLICATION

Prayer journal

DATE _____

TODAY'S PASSAGE   PREACHER   SERMON TOPIC

NOTES

| KEY VERSES |

| KEY POINTS |

PRAYER

| APPLICATION |

Prayer journal

DATE

TODAY'S PASSAGE   PREACHER   SERMON TOPIC

NOTES

KEY VERSES

PRAYER

KEY POINTS

APPLICATION

Made in the USA
Monee, IL
10 January 2022